TIPS FOR THE NEW MOM

ADD YOUR TIPS HERE:

Tiptionary Journals are a unique concept that combine selected tips from the best-selling book, **Tiptionary**, with space to write down all of those tips, shortcuts and ideas that have either been handed down to you from family and friends, or that you have discovered through "trial and error" along the way.

Tips for the New Mom takes a practical approach to offering helpful advice, by including those tips that are applicable to the new mother. We know that not every tip offered will be acted upon, nor should it be, but what we do offer is the opportunity to learn that there are many different ways to accomplish goals, cheaply and efficiently. When there's more than one way to achieve the same result, the tips you will find in this volume will help you make that choice.

The useful and practical tips you'll find in this book, combined with your own ideas and insights, will provide a valuable reference tool that will be used again and again, for years to come. And who knows? This may be the book that your children use later in their life when they want to find out, "How did Mom do that?"

The best thing about good advice is, it never goes out of style. So pass around this journal and pass on your best time and money-saving tips to the new mom!

BABY

BABY CARE • FEEDING • CLOTHES

BABY PRODUCTS

THE NEW BABY

Do not disturb!

Find the Do Not Disturb sign from your honeymoon hotel and use it on your front door. Or make a sign: Sssssh! Baby and Mommy are resting!

2 a.m. feedings

Make middle of the night bottle-fed feedings easier by filling a thermos jug with warm water and keeping it in the baby's room. Mix formula instantly instead of waiting at the stove for fifteen minutes. Also, have a snack ready for yourself.

Take it easy

Use paper plates and cups after you've first arrived home from the hospital to cut housework.

Answering machines

Let modern technology help you avoid answering the phone, especially when you've just arrived home with baby. Record the details of your baby's birth on the answering machine and add a message about when is the best time to call. (Remember, you should be sleeping when your baby is.)

OTHER TIPS

OTHER TIPS

_____

_____

_____

_____

_____

_____

_____

_____

_____

_____

_____

_____

_____

_____

_____

_____

_____

_____

_____

_____

_____

_____

_____

_____

_____

BABY CARE

Help baby to sleep

Tape-record the sound of a running dishwasher, a running shower or water filling the tub and play it back to lull your little one to sleep. The sound of running water simulates intrauterine sounds. Taping baby's own cries have also been known to work.

Relaxing at bath time

If you and your baby are both worn out, get in the tub together for a quiet break.

Fussy baby

Instead of taking your fussy baby for a car ride to calm her down, turn on the dryer and put baby securely in her baby carrier, then put the carrier on top of the dryer. The warmth of the dryer and gentle vibrating will soothe even the fussiest baby. Just remember to turn off the buzzer. An added bonus would be to time this with a laundry load that needs to be dried!

Bathing baby

Smear a tiny bit of petroleum jelly above baby's eyebrows to easily channel soapy water and shampoo away from eyes.

Bath safety

Wear cotton gloves on your hands for a better grip when holding and washing baby. Cover the faucet in the tub with a thick tube sock to protect baby from injury when bumping into it. Run the cold water last so that if your baby touches the faucet it won't be hot.

Bath seat/toy holder

Store your baby's bath toys in a five-gallon plastic bucket with drainage holes poked in the bottom. The bucket can stay in the tub between baths. When you empty the toys into the bath water, flip the bucket upside down to serve as a seat while you bathe baby.

OTHER TIPS

BABY CARE

Diaper rash

Rather than expensive diaper rash ointments, purchase store brand zinc oxide from the drugstore. It works great to prevent and treat diaper rash and is very inexpensive. Always consult your pediatrician about any unusual condition that does not clear up quickly.

Diaper rash prevention

Crisco™ is a great wetness barrier for babies, especially those in cloth diapers. Keeps skin soft and protects from diaper rash.

Baking soda bath

One-half cup baking soda in a warm bath is an excellent soother for diaper rash. Let the skin air dry after the bath and baby's bottom is on its way to well.

OTHER TIPS

Teething

To help your baby's discomfort try gently rubbing or massaging the gums with one of your fingers. Teething rings should be made of firm rubber (the teethers that you freeze tend to get too hard, and can cause more harm than good). Pain relievers and medications that you rub on the gums are not necessary or useful, either, since they wash out of the baby's mouth within minutes.

Baby teeth

To clean new teeth, brush them with a soft child's toothbrush, or wipe them with cotton swabs at the end of the day. To prevent cavities, never let your baby fall asleep with a bottle, either at nap time or at night. By avoiding this situation, you'll keep milk from pooling around the teeth and creating a breeding ground for decay.

OTHER TIPS

_____

_____

_____

_____

_____

_____

_____

_____

_____

_____

_____

_____

_____

_____

_____

_____

_____

_____

_____

_____

_____

_____

_____

_____

_____

_____

_____

_____

_____

_____

_____

BABY CARE

Trimming bangs

Paying an average of $10.00 just to have your little one's bangs trimmed seems unacceptable. Here's a great do-it-yourself tip: Place a piece of Scotch™ tape across the bangs and cut along the bottom edge. The tape keeps the hair nice and straight and you can step back and see if the tape placement is correct and straight before starting to cut. Bonus: Your little one just might be so curious about what you're doing that she'll sit still until you're done.

Shopping cart belt

Carry an extra belt in your car for shopping at stores that don't have child safety straps on their shopping cart seats. Fasten your baby in the cart seat with the belt.

OTHER TIPS

Sharing baby

When you must divide your attention between your baby and another child, give the child a doll and small diaper bag filled with inexpensive diapers, toys and a bottle. While you are taking care of your baby, the other child can take care of his/her own "baby."
Also allow the older child to help with caring for the baby, it helps with bonding between the children.

Quiet activity

Entertain bored little ones with bubbles. Keep a bottle in your diaper bag, purse or glove compartment and use it in the car, while waiting in line or at the doctor's office. Kids love to blow bubbles themselves or try to catch then, and even babies delight in this distraction.

OTHER TIPS

FEEDING

Private nursing

If you need to nurse your baby while out shopping, go to either the Children's or Women's department and ask to use a dressing room. You'll have a quiet and private nursing session, and after you are through your baby can look at herself in the mirror and play for a few minutes.

Bottle six-pack

Store bottles in the refrigerator in an empty cardboard six-pack bottle holder to keep them together and safe from tipping.

No more lost bottles

Do you leave baby bottles behind in friends' refrigerators after a visit? Try putting your car keys in the refrigerator with the bottles. You can't leave without them!

OTHER TIPS

Feeding baby

Avoid getting more baby food on your baby than in his mouth. Use a 1/2 to 1 teaspoon bulb medicine dropper. This is helpful when your six-month-old wants to knock a spoonful of food out of your hand and all over the both of you.

Two spoons for feeding

Use two spoons to make feeding your baby easier. If your baby has his own spoon, he'll quit trying to grab the one that you are using to feed him, and he may actually get some food inside his mouth!

Cook with a tea sieve

When preparing baby food, use a tea sieve to hold small pieces. This retains the flavors without allowing pieces into the food that may harm baby if swallowed.

Spit-up odor relief

Keep a spray bottle of water mixed with soda handy to clean up after baby's spit-up. This will keep the spot from setting and take away the odor.

OTHER TIPS

FEEDING

Breaking the bottle habit

To break your toddler from the bottle put powdered milk or buttermilk in the bottle or use Kool-Aid™ without the sugar added. Then put the milk or juice that your toddler loves in a sipper cup. Offer both to him and let him choose.

From bottle to cup

To help baby make the transition from bottle to cup, cut an "X" in the top of the nipple, invert it into the bottle, and insert a straw into the hole. This is an almost spill-proof drink holder. Your baby is already familiar with it and knows how to hold it.

Introducing new foods

The first time you try a new food on your baby only feed one spoonful. If your baby likes it and there is no adverse reaction, you might increase the amount at the next feeding. If your baby has had enough, do not coax him to eat more.

OTHER TIPS

Storing baby food

Remember that foods left over from a feeding should not be stored, so keep the initial portions small. If the baby's feeding spoon has been in the food at serving time, bacteria may grow if you store the leftovers.

Baby pizza

For babies who don't want to eat their own food anymore, cut a bagel in half and toast. Spread your baby's favorite baby food on face of bagel. He will love eating "pizza" just like mommy and daddy!!

High chair sliding

Keep your baby from sliding down in a high chair by putting a rubber sink mat or stick-on, non-slip bathtub daisies or strips on the seat.

Mealtime clean-up

Once your baby begins to feed herself at the table, give her a wet washcloth after eating. This will keep her busy washing herself, the high chair, and the table while you clean up, too.

OTHER TIPS

BABY CLOTHES

Disposable diapers

When choosing disposable diapers, consider the options. A super-absorbent diaper can lull you into thinking your baby doesn't need to be changed as often. And fewer diaper changes can mean more diaper rashes.

Changing diapers

When changing baby, place a clean diaper under baby's bottom. Undo soiled diaper, clean baby, then just secure clean diaper. The clean diaper that is placed underneath soiled one will help catch any little surprises. It's a quick and easy way to change your baby in a stroller or on the go without soiling the underneath surface.

OTHER TIPS

Security blankets

Many babies become attached to one special blanket. Make things easier for yourself by having two identical security blankets. This will allow you to wash one while the other is being used, thus sparing your baby (and yourself) a potential emotional crisis and a very bedraggled "lovey." If your baby has a large blanket, you can easily turn it into two by cutting it in half. He has little sense of size, and won't notice the change.

Receiving blankets

When your little one outgrows her tiny receiving blankets (or you still have yours from long ago!), sew them all together into a blanket for her to use either as a decoration or on her bed.

OTHER TIPS

BABY CLOTHES

Bibs on a budget

Make your bibs out of tablecloth material available at your fabric store for about $2.00 a yard. It is fuzzy on one side and nearly indestructible on the other. Use your favorite bib as a pattern. Place Velcro on the neck for closure (use self-adhesive if you don't sew) with the scratchy side facing away from baby's neck. No need to sew borders, it won't fray. If you have older kids, this material also makes great painting smocks

Baby formula stains

Unflavored meat tenderizer will remove some milk and baby formula stains from fabric. Make a paste of the tenderizer and cool water, rub on the spots, allow to sit, and wash as usual. The meat tenderizer contains an enzyme that breaks down the protein that is in milk and formula.

OTHER TIPS

Non-slip socks

Babies often slip when walking on linoleum or hardwood floors with just socks. Put fun designs on the bottom of your baby's socks with puff paint from a craft store to provide grip.

Less lacing

When first lacing up kids' new shoes, tie knots in the laces after the first two holes have been threaded, so your child can't pull them out accidentally.

OTHER TIPS

BABY PRODUCTS

Free baby products

Every month or so, call the toll-free numbers you find on diapers and other baby items to make a comment on the product and you'll be rewarded with a fistful of coupons.

Baby gift wrap

Wrap baby gifts in a receiving blanket, crib sheet, or hooded terry towel. Pin like a diaper with diaper pins.

Safe Toys

Infant toys, such as rattles, squeeze toys, and teethers, should be large enough so that they cannot enter and become lodged in an infant's throat.

Dangerous toys

Avoid crib and playpen toys, for example mobiles, with long, (20cm +) strings. Your infant can become entangled in such strings.

OTHER TIPS

Baby toy links

Shower curtain rings work perfectly for attaching baby toys to strollers, car seats, etc. At $1.29 for a package of 12, it's a great bargain.

Quiet baby toys

Purchase several colorful elastic "coiled" type key chain holders that will fit on your wrist. Make sure you remove the ring that holds the keys. When you want baby to stay quiet slip several of these elastic key chain bracelets on your wrist and let baby pull and snap away. They are soft and will not harm baby, and it will keep him fascinated for a long time pulling on them.

OTHER TIPS

_____
_____
_____
_____
_____
_____
_____
_____
_____
_____
_____
_____
_____
_____
_____
_____
_____
_____
_____
_____
_____
_____
_____
_____
_____
_____
_____
_____
_____

BABY PRODUCTS

Homemade baby wipes

You will need three cups of water, baby wash, baby lotion, and a thick roll of paper towels. Mix water with small amount of baby wash and baby lotion. Place paper towels in a container (one where the roll can stand upright is best). Pour the liquid solution onto the paper towels and let it soak in. Tear one sheet off at a time.

Extra uses for diaper wipes

Use to quickly clean shoes before a party or pictures. They work great at taking washable crayon marks off of walls, toys, phones, laminated books, etc. Let toddlers "wash" their toys and dolls when they get dirty. To wash little one's hands, let them wipe first with a diaper wipe, then rub and rinse in the water. They also work to pre-clean adult's hands after dirty work. Saves some wear and tear on the towels.

OTHER TIPS

Diaper pail

To clean a foul smelling diaper pail, fill the pail with a solution of one cup liquid chlorine bleach to each gallon of hot water, and soak overnight. Empty the pail into the toilet or bathtub, rinse it out, and rub the inside with a paste of baking soda and water; let stand overnight. In the morning, rinse the pail. To prevent odors from returning, change water often and sprinkle the pail with baking soda.

Diaper pins

Store diaper pins in a bar of soap (safely away from curious hands). When ready for use they will slide so easily through the diaper.

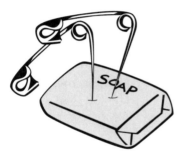

OTHER TIPS

BABY PRODUCTS

Bedding

When choosing a mattress, be sure to check it is made with non-flammable materials. Keep your baby warm with layers of lightweight bedding to maintain air flow.

Cribs

If you use a crib made before 1985, make sure that slats are no more than 2 3/8 inches apart, and there are no cutouts in the headboard or footboard. As soon as your baby can sit, lower the mattress of the crib to the level where he cannot fall out. As soon as your child can pull to a standing position, remove crib bumpers as well as anything large enough to be used as a step for climbing out.

Squeaky crib rails

Apply petroleum jelly or spray nonstick vegetable oil to the side rails of the crib to keep them from squeaking when they're raised or lowered. Or rub them with waxed paper.

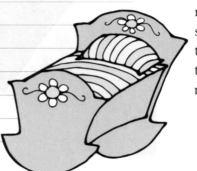

OTHER TIPS

Dry crib sheets

Use a rubberized flannel lap
pad (pieces available in fabric
stores) over crib sheets to avoid
having to disturb your baby by
changing sheets after every
leak and spit-up.

Bassinet pad

Cover your bassinet pad with a
standard pillowcase. Then just
flip it over for a dry, fresh side
when needed.

Used changing table

Replace the outdated pattern
on the top with a new shower
curtain. Cut to fit, and attach
with staples to the back. Or,
use receiving blankets.

Changing fun & safety

Hang a large mirror on the wall
next to your baby's changing
table. Baby will love looking at
your reflection in the mirror,
and this may be where you
witness his first smile or laugh.
Your baby will naturally turn in
that direction during changing,
and will roll towards the wall
and safety, not off the table.

OTHER TIPS

BABY PRODUCTS

Clean sippy-lids

Tempted to throw out those crusty lids to your kid's sippy cups? Try this: A brush for cleaning cake-decorating tips fits perfectly. And, they usually cost under a dollar!

Baby bottle rack

Baby bottles and their various parts take up a lot of counter space while drying. An easy solution is to hang one of those three-tiered wire vegetable baskets over the sink. The bottom basket is for bottles, the next basket for nipples, and the top can be used for sippy cup lids or bibs.

Baby gate bargain

Baby-proof your home with "pet gates" purchased at a pet super store rather than paying the premium price for baby gates. You end up paying a lot less for gates of identical quality.

OTHER TIPS

Carpeted playpen

Use a carpet remnant to fit the floor of your child's playpen. It keeps baby warmer and it's easy to remove for cleaning.

Pet-proofing

You can "pet proof" the baby's room by putting a gate across the door or by installing a screen door. You'll still be able to see in the room and pets will be kept out. To help your family dog or cat adjust to the new baby, bring home one of the baby's diapers or blankets the day before your baby is brought home and give it to your pet to play with and sniff. The baby's odor will then be familiar to your pet.

OTHER TIPS

BABY PRODUCTS

Substitute playpen

Use a small inflatable plastic wading pool as a playpen for a baby who's not yet actively crawling. There are no rough edges and the pool is usually colorfully decorated. After the baby begins to crawl, the pool is still useful as a mat for under the high chair to catch food. Then in the summer you still have a pool. Not bad for a couple of dollars!

Baby pool bath

Filling up a whole tub seems to be a waste of water when you have a baby. Instead, use an inflatable baby pool, small enough to put in the tub without it crinkling. Just remember to put in a few non-slip stickers and never leave the baby alone.

FAMILY

CHILDREN • CLOTHING • SPECIAL TIMES
MEDICAL • PERSONAL CARE

CHILDREN

OTHER TIPS

Babysitter checklist

In addition to your rules and emergency contacts, write down your child-care secrets (bed-time routine, feeding schedule, favorite toys or songs).

While you're away

Leave a loaded camera or camcorder with your babysitter so that the next time your child does something new and special, you won't have to miss it.

Parent duty

To avoid bed-time conflicts, teach your toddler to share parents. Make a colorful drawing of your child's bed and put it on your refrigerator. Each day rotate a photo of Mom or Dad on the drawing. This shows your child who will put him to bed that evening.

Bed-time stories

To make bedtime easier, make up stories with your child as the leading character. The story ends with the hero falling asleep.

OTHER TIPS

CHILDREN

Kids' memories scrapbook

Buy 8 1/2" by 11" sheet protectors, an inexpensive binder, and some sheets that are designed for holding pictures of various sizes. Whenever you get a new memento, slip it into the next empty sheet protector. Date and describe the kids' artwork on the back. Birthday cards can be grouped together and share one protector. The plastic page covers let kids touch without making fingerprints and new items are automatically put in chronological order.

Picture book

Take a small photo album and fill it with photos of people your child knows (family, pets) and people she doesn't see often (grandparents, etc.). If you label the pictures it can be used when reading starts.

OTHER TIPS

Birthday video

Every year on your child's birthday why not make a ten-minute video comprised of various photos of them from the past year with music dubbed in. Simply pick music you like (or your little one liked that year) and time its length. Then pick out the photos you want in the video and record each one (about four seconds per photo is right) until you've recorded enough to equal the length of the music. Your camcorder owner's manuel will explain how to add music. Record each child's year on their own tape and give them their 'Life Story' when they turn 18.

OTHER TIPS

CHILDREN

Double-decked closet

In the children's closets, install a high clothes rod for seldom-worn dress clothes and a lower one for everyday items. The lower one should be positioned low enough so the child can easily reach it.

Prevent a lock-in

Toss a towel over the top of a bathroom door so it won't close completely. This way, little ones are less likely to lock themselves in.

Liquid hand soap for kids

If your small children are really into washing their hands and go fairly nuts with the soap dispenser, make up a special batch of handwashing soap just for them: Mix 10 parts liquid dishwashing detergent or generic shampoo to one part water.

OTHER TIPS

Fresh toys

To freshen up a stuffed animal or doll that can't be laundered, give the toy a "shower" with baking soda. Sprinkle it on, work it in, allow to sit for a while, then shake well or vacuum the baking soda away.

Toddler toys

Save up all the toys from the kids' meals and stuff them in their Christmas stockings.

Puzzles for toddlers

Glue bright-colored pictures from magazines or books onto pieces of cardboard. When dry, draw lines shaped like puzzle pieces over the picture. Cut the pieces out and teach little ones how to put together.

OTHER TIPS

CHILDREN

Preserving crayons

To prolong the life of a new box of crayons, wrap transparent tape around the outside of each crayon. This will make them really strong and resistant to breakage. Sharpen as usual.

Crayon graffiti

Tape butcher paper along the lower area of a wall as your child's giant canvass. If your little one creates something spectacular, you can cut off the area and save it for posterity.

Giant chalkboard

For a fun and inexpensive way to add to a playroom, buy a can of chalkboard paint for about $5.00. Paint a wall (takes eight hours to dry). It is a great way to personalize a room, encourage creativity, teach the alphabet or numbers and to let your kids draw on the wall!

OTHER TIPS

Telephone toys

If it seems like every time you get on the telephone your little one "needs" you, keep a large bag of small toys hidden until it's "telephone time!" Children get so excited when their "new" toys appear out of nowhere (usually the closet), and Mom can have a nice conversation.

Wading pool

To keep a child from slipping in a plastic wading pool, affix nonslip adhesive shapes for a bathtub to the bottom.

OTHER TIPS

CLOTHING

Clothing sizes

When you see a great sale on kids' clothes, don't you wish you could know what size your kids will be next winter or summer so you can stock up on larger sizes? Here's a great way to make a prediction: Ask your kids' doctor for a children's height/weight chart. Now plot your children's weights and heights for the past year or so and follow the growth line to get a very good idea of how they will grow in the next year.

Clothing swap

Arrange a clothing swap with friends. Ask everyone to bring at least five items in good condition that no longer fit, flatter, or meet their needs. One person's disaster could be your delight.

Fresh clothing

To keep children's clothes from having that "musty" smell from being stored away all winter or summer, put a fabric softener dryer sheet in the bottom of storage container. This keeps clothes smelling fresh all season.

OTHER TIPS

Declutter

Use suitcases and pack each child's off-season clothes in them. Store the suitcases in their now-tidy closets.

Replacement guarantee

Sears has a nationwide policy regarding children's clothing, sizes newborn through 16. If any item wears out, upon return it will be replaced in the same size, color, and style at absolutely no additional cost. There is no time frame rule that says you must be the original owner, or that limits the number of times an item can be replaced. The only requirement is that it must be identifiable as a Sears product, so don't remove labels. This policy is known as Sears' Replacement Guarantee.

OTHER TIPS

_____
_____
_____
_____
_____
_____
_____
_____
_____
_____
_____
_____
_____
_____
_____
_____
_____
_____
_____
_____
_____
_____
_____
_____
_____
_____
_____
_____
_____
_____
_____

CLOTHING

Swimsuits

To prolong the life of swimsuits that are exposed to harsh chlorine, buy a bottle of chlorine remover, sold in pet supply stores for removing chlorine from the water in fish tanks. Add a few drops of the liquid to a pail of cold water, pop the suits in when you are done swimming, and follow with a cold tap water rinse.

Zipper troubles

To get stubborn, sluggish metal zippers back into shape, run the lead of an ordinary pencil along the zipper's teeth to lubricate them. Or, with a cotton swab, apply a bit of lubricating spray such as WD-40™ to the teeth. Or, rub the edge of a bar of soap or an old candle up and down the teeth and along both sides of the zipper.

Button security

Buttons on new clothes often fall off after just one wearing and washing. Before you wear a new item, cover the thread on each button with clear nail polish or a drop of Super Glue™.

SPECIAL TIMES

Progressive party

Instead of everyone in your circle of friends hosting a separate holiday party, have a progressive dinner. The party moves from one house to another, with hors d'oeuvres at the first stop, appetizer at the second, main course at the next, and dessert and coffee at the last. It's an enjoyable way to share the burden and you get to see everyone's holiday decorations too.

Christmas charity

Several weeks before Christmas help your children go through their toys, picking out those they'd like to give to others. Even toddlers can grasp the concept of giving and sharing, if you give them the power to decide and include them in the delivery to a shelter. Or, have your kids leave some of their old toys for Santa to take on the rest of his journey. Once the kids are asleep, hide the toys so you can deliver them to a worthy charity.

OTHER TIPS

OTHER TIPS

SPECIAL TIMES

Christmas book

Start a family Christmas book, adding your favorite memories each year. At the beginning of the holiday season, pull out the book and go through the pages with your little ones.

Christmas ornaments

Collect ornaments for your child and use them as place-cards at the holiday meal. They will have a wonderful collection for their first "adult" Christmas tree and it's a fun way of recalling childhood memories.

Holiday mantelpiece

To make a gorgeous yet cheap holiday mantelpiece, lay sprays of evergreens on the mantelpiece with a string of white lights, and add some of your collectables, ornaments, or pinecones amid the greens.

OTHER TIPS

Free concerts

Most cities have community or church sponsored entertainment during holidays and summer months. Make it a habit to check the paper and community bulletin board for local events. If tickets to a special concert or play are out of your price range, ask if you can attend a rehearsal.

Field trips

Many interesting factories offer tours. Call the chamber of commerce in the cities you will be visiting on your next family vacation for a listing of all the factories that offer tours. While you're at it, keep a list of the ones in your own area. Typically these kinds of tours include free samples of the factory's product.

Go to college

Local colleges often show movies in a setting that's better than some small theaters and at a much lower cost.

OTHER TIPS

SPECIAL TIMES

Skip first-run films

All but the biggest blockbusters are available on video three months after release. Your patience will pay off. Or, go to a movie matinee. It's always cheaper.

Cheap tickets

If you enjoy cultural events or visiting local museums and theaters, volunteer as an usher or ticket collector or to fill some other need. In exchange you will probably receive free or reduced admissions. Ask about the policy ahead of time.

Mirror notes

Leave a reminder for family members by writing notes on the bathroom mirror with a dry erase marker, available in all kinds of colors at office supply stores. It wipes right off with a tissue, and it's sure to be seen. If a note is left unerased for some time, use a bit of rubbing alcohol on that tissue to wipe it away without a trace.

MEDICAL

Ask questions

Seventy-five percent of all antibiotics taken each year are unnecessary. Doctors know that patients who take the time and trouble to make an office visit expect to be "rewarded" with a prescription. Doctors like to keep their patients happy too. Ask the prescribing doctor exactly what the prescription can and cannot do for you and if it is necessary for full recovery.

Cash discount

Whenever undergoing a dental or medical procedure for which you will eventually pay, inquire about a cash discount. Do not be timid about expecting as much as 25 percent discount when you pay by check or cash at the time the procedure is done. Never be afraid to ask.

OTHER TIPS

OTHER TIPS

MEDICAL

Emergency rooms

Avoid emergency facilities unless you have a true medical emergency on your hands. As a rule, you should call your family doctor first in time of crisis. If that is not possible, use a 24-hour emergency clinic before considering the hospital's emergency room.

Hospital bills

Carefully examine hospital bills even if you have full insurance coverage. Hospitals are known for making mistakes, and a good consumer scrutinizes every charge. Report all discrepancies to the hospital, physician, and insurance company.

Immunizations

Keep kids' immunizations up-to-date. Look for free or cheap immunization programs through your local health department. Having sick kids sometimes means that parents must miss work or pay for expensive alternative day care. The cost really can add up.

OTHER TIPS

Shot distraction

Distract and minimize discomfort while your little one is getting a shot by bringing along a paper party blower for him or her to use.

Physician samples

Every doctor's office is flooded with all kinds of expensive prescription samples, also known as "stock bottles." When required to take a medication, be sure to ask your doctor if he or she might have samples for you to try. Asking for sufficient samples to make sure the medication is right for you is especially wise, particularly if you might be allergic to it. Don't hesitate to ask again every time you come to the office. Doctors can even write a prescription for a stock bottle to be filled at the pharmacy for patients unable to afford the prescription.

OTHER TIPS

MEDICAL

Generic equivalents

Ask for generic prescriptions, which cost up to 50 percent less, yet by law must have the same chemical makeup and potency. Also, buy generic non-prescription pain medication. Advil™ costs about $8.00 for 100 tablets, while ibuprofen (active ingredient in Advil™) costs about $2.00. The same goes for Tylenol™, which is acetaminophen. Consult the pharmacist when in doubt.

Kids' medications

Don't use tableware spoons when giving medicine to a child. Spoons in your silverware drawer may not hold the correct amount of liquid. A spoon that's off by even one milliliter could mean you're giving the child 20 percent more or less of the dose. Use a proper measuring device such as a measuring spoon, syringe, oral dropper, etc. Ask the pharmacist for a complimentary calibrated measuring device.

OTHER TIPS

No more spilled medicine

When giving your baby medicine, sit on the floor with your legs out straight with her on her back between your legs, just closed enough so she can't move her head. Now she is immobile and both your hands are still free; one to pry open her mouth and the other to stick the dropper in her mouth.

Split those tablets

If your doctor prescribes, for example, 50 milligrams (mg) dosage tablets, ask about changing that to the 100 mg version so you can break the tablets in two to accomplish the 50 mg dosage. You will save a lot of money because the difference in price between 100 mg and 50 mg will usually be negligible. A tablet splitter costs just a few dollars at any pharmacy. Caution: Some pills' delivery systems may be affected by splitting them in half. Check with your doctor or pharmacist first.

OTHER TIPS

MEDICAL

Oatmeal bath

If your children get chicken pox, and an oatmeal bath is in order, save a lot of money by making your own oatmeal bath product similar to Aveeno™. Take old-fashioned rolled oats and a clean, old knee-high nylon. Place a handful of the oats into the stocking, tie a knot in the end, and let it sit in the bath water. Squish it with your hand to activate it more quickly.

Vitamin C

Vitamin C works in the body as a scavenger, picking up all sorts of trash, including virus trash. It can shorten the length of a cold from seven days to two or three. It has been proven to lower cholesterol, decrease arthritis pain, reduce outbreaks of canker sores, and lessen premenstrual syndrome.

PERSONAL CARE

Calcium

Don't drink sodas together with calcium rich foods or supplements. If your soft drink contains phosphoric acid, it will block absorption of calcium into the bloodstream.

Cosmetics

If you love a particular high-priced cosmetic line, inquire as to the name of their economy line. For example, Lancome™ (available in department stores) also produces the L'Oreal™ line (available in any drugstore). Call the customer service department of your favorite line to inquire.

Eye makeup remover

Use a no-tears type baby shampoo to remove eye makeup. Ophthamologists encourage contact lens wearers to do this to reduce protein buildup on their lenses. Apply with a cotton swab in a brushing motion while holding eyelid taut. Rinse.

OTHER TIPS

OTHER TIPS

PERSONAL CARE

Foot massage

Give your tired feet a mini-massage by rolling them back and forth over an icy cold soda or juice can.

Health clubs

Try the club before you join. Most offer several free visits or short, low-cost trial memberships. Join with a group of five or so friends, and at some clubs you'll save as much as 35 percent. Pay a year's dues in advance and save up to 20 percent (make sure the club has a reasonable likelihood of still being in business a year from now). Ask about new member perquisites, such as a free session with a personal trainer. Also, if you need to take a long-term break for travel or other reasons, ask the club to freeze your membership and start it up again upon return.

Herbal bath

There's nothing like a relaxing, naturally scented bath to revive a tired mind and body. Fill a piece of cheesecloth with fresh rosemary, tie it up with string, hang the bag from the faucet, and fill the tub.

Petroleum jelly

Apply a small amount of petroleum jelly to your skin nightly. It's a natural moisturizer and is especially effective on extra dry areas like elbows, heels, and knees.

Shampoo

Don't be a shampoo snob. In a 1992 *Consumer Reports* test of 132 brand-name shampoos, the lowly cheap brands from the supermarket rated just as high as the pricey salon brands.

OTHER TIPS

OTHER TIPS

PERSONAL CARE

Skin care products

A reader asked a doctor friend what he learned during his dermatology rotation concerning expensive skin and facial cleansing products. He informed her that the best products are not the most expensive. Dermatologists recommend Dove™ or Lever 2000™ for cleansing and Lubriderm™ lotion for moisturizing. Both products are sold over the counter at any drug and most grocery stores.

Tired feet

Freshen tired feet and soften skin easily and quickly. Add four tablespoons of baking soda to one quart of warm water. Pour into a large container, and let your footsies soak in it for 10 minutes.

HOME

DECORATING • CLEANING
LAUNDRY • COOKING • GROCERIES

DECORATING

Fragrant home

Here are several ideas for a home, sweet, home:
(1) Sprinkle cinnamon on a pan and warm it on the stove.
(2) For a citrus aroma, throw a handful of orange peels in a pot of boiling water. (3) Each time you clean a room, place a few drops of a fragrant oil on a light bulb, or spray with a fresh potpourri scent to leave a subtle sign that this room is clean! (4) To make your own carpet and room deodorizer, mix one cup Epsom™ salts with a few drops of perfumed oil. Spread on waxed paper to dry. Store in an airtight container. To use, sprinkle the grains on the carpet, allow to stand for a few minutes, and vacuum as usual. (5) Put a cinnamon stick in the vacuum bag before vacuuming for a natural deodorizer. (6) Don't throw away lemon rinds or old spices; they make fabulous room deodorizers. Simply place them in a pot of water and bring to a low boil. The scent is better than any potpourri you can buy.

OTHER TIPS

OTHER TIPS

DECORATING

Hang a picture

This is a formula that professional picture hangers use: (1) Measure up 60 inches from the floor. (2) To this, add half the height of the framed picture. (3) Subtract the height of the wire (the height of the triangle that the wire would form if the frames were actually hanging in place). This magic number is the distance from the floor at which you should nail the picture hook regardless of the height of the ceiling or even your height.

Hanging on wallpaper

To hang pictures on wallpaper: Cut a notch in the paper, bend it back gently, then drive the nail into the wall. If you remove the nail later, you can simply glue the paper flap over the hole, and there won't be an ugly blemish on the paper.

OTHER TIPS

Kids art

Transfer a child's artwork to fabric to make into a pillow or wall hanging for their own room, or another. For babies, make feet and handprints on lamp shades, comforters or pillows and decorate their room.

Displaying artwork

Can't bear to part with your toddler's artwork, yet don't have enough refrigerator space to display it? Decorate the garage! Staple them with a staple gun to the walls in your garage. Your little one will be so proud and your neighbors will get a kick out of it, too.

Decorator album

Fill a purse-size photo album with paint, fabric, and wallpaper samples organized by room. Take the album when you go shopping or to garage sales, and you'll take the guesswork out of finding coordinating accessories for your home.

OTHER TIPS

DECORATING

Negatives in safekeeping

To save precious memories in the event of a future house fire or some other horrible disaster that would destroy your family photograph collection, take some negatives from each year's pictures, and put them in your safe-deposit box.

Reference tips

Photograph room arrangements to use as a reference when you rehang and resettle everything in your new home. When you finish decorating a room, write down this information and tape it to the back of the switch plate: the brand and color of the paint, how many rolls of wallpaper were used, and the circuit breaker number that serves this room.

Socket protectors

Decorate unsightly socket protectors by gluing wooden shapes to them (such as hearts) and paint them to match your decor.

OTHER TIPS

Quilt tablecloth

A baby-size quilt draped over a plain table rather than being hidden in a drawer can give a room an instant "face-lift".

Drawer organizer

Keep your earrings, small bracelets, and necklaces in the separate compartments of a plastic ice tray. The tray fits in a dresser drawer so jewels stay neat and out of reach of little fingers.

Baby food jar organizer

Attach the lids of empty baby food jars with a nail to a beam in your basement or garage workshop. Fill jars with nails, screws, or any other small items. Screw the jars onto the lids. The clear jars allow you to easily see the part you want, and they are so easy to remove and replace.

OTHER TIPS

CLEANING

Baby bottle cleaners

Use a dab of toothpaste with your bottle brush and just enough water to scrub it clean.

Glass bottle cleaner

Try denture cleaner tablets to clean glass baby bottles. Let the bottles soak for a half-hour according to directions. Swish with a bottle brush and rinse.

Baking soda

Baking soda is a nonabrasive cleanser. Use it without worry on fine china, porcelain appliances, the inside of the refrigerator, stainless steel, aluminum, and cast iron. You can use it either in its powdered form or mix it with water to make a paste.

Odor absorbent

If you want to remove an offensive odor, think baking soda. Keep an open, shallow dish of baking soda behind your toilet to absorb odors.

Crayon marks on floors and walls

Get rid of crayon marks from a linoleum floor by rubbing lightly with a dab of silver polish. To remove your child's crayon marks from painted walls, dip a damp cloth into baking soda and rub the spot gently.

Carpet stains

Rubbing alcohol is an easy and inexpensive spot remover for carpets. Lightly rub a drop or two of alcohol into the stain, then blot the spot dry with a clean, white cloth.

Grease marks on wallpaper

Remove a grease spot from wallpaper by rubbing baby powder into it. This serves as an absorbent.

OTHER TIPS

OTHER TIPS

CLEANING

Glass shower doors

Mineral oil will remove
stubborn scum from the inside
of glass shower doors. Give
the tiles, faucets, and outside of
shower door a final once-over
with glass cleaner to make
them really shine.

Chrome

A quick and easy cleaner for
chrome is baby oil sprinkled on
a damp cloth.

Mildew

Here's a way to get rid of
mildew buildup in your shower
stall without using harsh,
household bleach: Fill an
empty spray bottle with vinegar
and a cup of salt. Spray the
stall, allow the solution to sit
for at least a half-hour,
and then rinse thoroughly.
Tougher jobs may require a
second application.

OTHER TIPS

Leaking toilet

Find the water leaks. Give your home this test: Turn off all running water in the house. Find your water meter and take a look. Is it still moving? Chances are you have a water leak, and chances are even better it's your toilet. Put a few drops of food coloring into the toilet's tank. If without flushing, the color shows up in the bowl, it's leaking, all right. Get a toilet repair kit at the home repair center. This is a very simple do-it-yourself repair.

Toilet cleaner

If your toilet bowl has really stubborn stains, drop one or two denture cleaning tablets into the bowl and allow to sit overnight. Brush and flush.

OTHER TIPS

LAUNDRY

Dryer sheets

Tear dryer sheets in half to get more life out of them; they will still soften a whole load of laundry. Then, save the used dryer sheets. They make great dusting and cleaning cloths for television and computer screens. Not only will they clean the screens, the antistatic properties will treat the screens to repel rather than attract dust.

No hassle laundry

To make sorting clean laundry less of a hassle, have a separate laundry basket for each member of the family. Let kids pick out which color they want and decorate it. Each family member is responsible for putting away their clothes.

Sock sorting

Let young children help separate and match clean socks. This chore is great for teaching about pairs, colors, and encourages positive self esteem.

Baby shampoo for delicates

Instead of using expensive cold-water detergents for delicates and fine sweaters, use baby shampoo. The results will be the same, and the cost is considerably less.

Laundering diapers

When laundering diapers, use borax instead of bleach. Bleach wears down the fabric and your diapers will be in shreds within a year. After the entire cycle, rinse again; add one cup vinegar to the final rinse to remove every last bit of soap. Drying diapers outdoors in the sun sterilizes them further and saves even more money.

OTHER TIPS

OTHER TIPS

LAUNDRY

Stain recipe

This recipe will get out baby stains, even those on which you'd given up hope after many washings and dryings. Fill a large bucket or container with the hottest tap water available. Add 1/2 cup Clorox II™ and 1/2 cup Cascade™ Automatic Dishwasher Powder for each gallon of water. Submerge stained items. Allow to soak at least three hours, preferably overnight.

Ink stains

Aerosol hairsprays, because they contain a high concentration of acetone, will remove some ballpoint ink stains from clothing. Try this: Hold a rag under the fabric to blot the ink that comes through on the other side, then aim and spray. Another quick, easy, and cheap way to get ink spots out of washable clothing is to soak the stain in milk. Wash as usual.

OTHER TIPS

Presoaked stains

If you have an infant or toddler who sometimes soils a garment while you are away from home, try this trick to keep the stain from setting. Put two tablespoons of powdered Dreft™ and one tablespoon of Biz™ in a gallon size zip-type bag and keep it in your diaper bag. If a garment is soiled, simply put the garment in the bag, add water, seal the bag and shake to mix everything together. When you get home, the garment has been presoaked and is ready to wash.

Gentle stain remover

Place small pieces of Ivory™ soap inside an an orphan hosiery knee high, knot securely. Toss it in the wash with baby's clothes. It will keep clothes looking cleaner. You can also rub Ivory™ soap on spit up stains before washing to help remove the stain.

OTHER TIPS

LAUNDRY

More stain removers

The following household items will get rid of most stains, but the real trick is to treat stains as soon as possible. Don't let them sit in the hamper. Clean sneakers with a soap filled scouring pad. Add lemon juice or bleach to the rinse water if the shoes are white. Chocolate or grape juice can be cleaned with club soda. Rub it in until the stain is gone and then wash as usual. Food coloring stains can be rubbed with toothpaste. Let dry then rinse in cold water. Launder as usual. Apply hydrogen peroxide to blood stains, then soak in cold water for 30 minutes or more. Grass stains can be treated with a solution of one part alcohol to two parts water. Boil white, dirt-stained socks in water with a sliced lemon.

COOKING

Mealtime fun

Make eating at home fun!
- Rearrange your eating area
- Make a new tablecloth
- Use place mats
- Play background music
- Light some candles
- Have a picnic in your family room

Mealtime entertainment

To occupy a baby or toddler during mealtimes, provide finger foods or kitchen items like measuring cups, plastic strainers, or margarine tubs with lids. Take plastic measuring spoons, fan them out in front of the child, and place a piece of toasted oat cereal in each spoon. Kids love it, and it seems to be a good exercise in dexterity.

OTHER TIPS

OTHER TIPS

COOKING

Frozen baby food

Puree some of the family's regular food in the blender. Pour into ice trays, freeze, pop "food cubes" into large freezer bags, keep frozen until needed, and simply heat them in the microwave. Smoothing Saran Wrap™ over the ice cube trays before freezing reduces ice crystals and freezer burn.

Frozen snacks

Keep marshmallows, potato chips, pretzels, and crackers in the freezer. They are best if frozen in their original unopened containers. This trick works well for popcorn kernels, too. They will stay fresh much longer, and freezing will encourage every kernel to pop.

Punch cubes

Freeze whatever drink you are serving in an ice cube tray ahead of time. Drinks will stay chilled and won't get all watered down.

OTHER TIPS

Baby bottles on ice

When packing up a cooler, forget the bags of ice and expensive cold packs. Fill an old plastic baby bottle with water, screw the cap on very tightly, and freeze. It won't leak water like ice and it's cheaper than cold packs.

Fresh bananas

If you keep bananas in a closed plastic bag, they will keep at least two weeks on your counter.

Citrus fruit spray

Fill a spray bottle with lemon-lime soft drink to spray on apple and banana slices to prevent them from turning brown.

Colorful food

Solve the problem of boring food by adding a few drops of food coloring to your little one's oatmeal, pancakes, or eggs.

OTHER TIPS

COOKING

Baking for a family

When baking more than one item at a time, make sure there's plenty of room between the pans, walls, and racks of the oven for air to circulate.

Cake cooling

To cool a cake that has just come out of the oven, place the pan on a wet towel. The cake is less likely to stick to the pan if it's cooled this way.

Cake writing like a pro

Use a toothpick to sketch letters onto a frosted cake before you try to write "Happy Birthday" or another message with icing. If you make a mistake, smooth the top and start again. When you're happy with your lettering, simply apply icing along the sketched lines.

OTHER TIPS

Cake decorator

A clean, squeezable mustard bottle is great for decorating cakes. Just fill it with the color you want, screw on the pointed tip, and get to work on that cake.

Creative Birthday Cake

Avoid the expense of purchasing themed birthday cakes. Find a birthday card with an image you like, and cut it out with enough of a base to insert into the frosted cake top. Then add background decorations with frosting, such as a picture of a dalmation with chocolate paw prints all over a white cake and red trim. After the cake is served, cut off the base of the picture and put it in a scrapbook with the birthday photos. (PS. don't put the candles right next to the card picture!)

OTHER TIPS

COOKING

Heart-shaped cake

No special pan is required for this cake. Just bake one round layer and one square layer, cool and remove from pans. On a large tray, platter, or foil covered cardboard, place the square layer with corners pointing up, down, right, and left so it looks like a diamond. Slice the round layer into two equal halves. Place a half on two adjacent sides of the square layer.

Cookies

A thin coat of nonstick vegetable spray on cookie cutters will prevent dough from sticking to the metal. This also works with your children's play dough. You can also put a slice of bread in the cookie jar to absorb the moisture that causes cookies to become stale.

Applesauce trick

When baking, cut down on or omit the amount of butter or margarine used by substituting applesauce. Use one tablespoon of applesauce per cup of flour.

OTHER TIPS

Brownies

For extra-fudgy brownies, add one tablespoon corn syrup to the batter, either a box mix or from scratch. Bake as usual. Also, don't assume it always pays to bake from scratch. Brownies, for example, are often cheaper to make from a mix.

Cupcakes

To keep plastic wrap from sticking to cupcakes (and other homemade frosted treats), spray the plastic wrap with some nonstick cooking spray. The cupcakes will arrive at their destination with frosting intact.

OTHER TIPS

GROCERIES

One pound equivalents

The following amounts are equal to one pound: 2 cups butter; 2 1/3 cups white granulated sugar; 2 cups packed brown sugar; 3 3/4 cups confectioners' sugar; 3 1/2 cups all-purpose flour; 4 cups cake flour; 3 3/4 cups whole wheat flour; 4 cups cocoa; 3 cups loosely packed raisins; 2 3/4 cups sliced apples; 2 cups fresh pitted cherries; 5 cups sliced, fresh mushrooms; 3 cups sliced white potatoes.

Generic

Some generic grocery items are exactly the same as the more expensive brand-name version. By law, certain items, such as aspirin, baking soda, cornstarch, honey, molasses, peanuts, pecans, salt, sugar, unbleached flour, and walnuts must be exactly the same content and composition, regardless of packaging or quantity gimmicks.

OTHER TIPS

Bargains

Search for bargains in the day-old baked goods, dented can, and "meat that is about to expire" bins. You have to be careful, but as long as the cans are not bulging or leaking and the appearance and dates meet your approval, go for it. Also look for generic and off-brands for additional savings.

Discontinued products

Today's grocery stores will only carry those items that move well in order to maintain their profit margin. Watch for product shelf labels with either a line drawn through the price code numbers or the letters "DC" or "Discontinued" written on them. By purchasing these "unadvertised" specials, you will often find savings of at least 20 percent or more on your register tape.

OTHER TIPS

GROCERIES

Meat shelf life

Never purchase more meat than you can properly refrigerate and reasonably use within the following periods of time: Ground beef and beef cut into small pieces, such as stew meat, should be used within two days of purchase. Steak should be used within four days of purchase, and roast should be used within one week. If you cannot comply, be sure to freeze as soon as possible.

Dairy

The date on dairy products is the date when retailers must pull unsold products from the shelf. Properly stored, the product will be good for at least seven days past the printed date.

Milk substitution

For toddler eaters, substitute vanilla ice cream when you're out of milk. It works well with waffles and hot cereal.

FINANCES

ANKING • PURCHASES • GIFT GIVING
FAMILY CAR • TRAVEL

BANKING

Make savings a regular bill

Once a month, or whenever you pay your bills, write a check to deposit in your money market fund or your savings account. If you can't start with 10 percent, start with less and increase the amount each month. Use automatic savings plans; let the bank take your savings out of your paycheck. You won't miss what you don't see.

Check for deposits

Usually if you have been a good customer of the utility companies (gas, water, electricity, phone) for at least a year, you can arrange to have your deposits refunded or credited toward your account. You may be able to get interest, too, if you ask.

OTHER TIPS

OTHER TIPS

BANKING

Audit long-distance bills

Have your phone bill audited by several long-distance providers. Some long-distance companies offer auditing services at no charge. You send them several monthly bills, and they determine what you would have paid had you used their service. If you decide to switch, make sure all fees to make the move will be waived and that you can go back if you are unsatisfied with the new service.

Pay annually

If possible, pay insurance premiums annually. Avoid the added costs for monthly or quarterly billing.

OTHER TIPS

Life insurance for kids

Don't buy life insurance for kids. It makes absolutely no sense. Insure only wage earners (including stay home moms) whose untimely demise would create a financial hardship.

Homeowner's insurance

Ask about homeowner's insurance discounts for security systems, smoke alarms, and good driving records. The agent or company may not volunteer the information.

Renter's insurance

If you rent, buy a tenant's policy. Landlords are not responsible for your belongings in case of disaster.

OTHER TIPS

BANKING

Buying a bargain property

If you're looking for a bargain, buy the worst house in a good neighborhood. You can always fix up a house, but you can't change the neighborhood.

Interest on earnest money

When purchasing a home, make sure you will earn interest on your deposit during the escrow period.

Property taxes

Challenge your property tax bill. If declined, you might be entitled to a reassessment of your taxes.

OTHER TIPS

Know what you have

Call the Social Security Administration at 800-772-1213 for a "Request for Earnings and Benefits Estimate Statement." After you mail back the completed form, you will receive a statement showing all the money you have paid into social security as well as a personalized estimated monthly benefit upon retirement. If there are errors, they can be corrected, but only if you report them.

New deduction

To claim your baby as a tax deduction for the current year, the child must have a Social Security number. To apply, call 1-800-772-1213. Apply for your child's number as soon as possible. In many hospitals, when the baby's birth is registered, the hospital will also provide you with the necessary form at no charge.

OTHER TIPS

PURCHASES

Warranties

Buy a large three-ring binder and a supply of plastic pocket inserts. Whenever you purchase a product, whether it's appliance, lawn tool, or toy, staple the receipt to the owner's manual or warranty paperwork and file it away in one of the pockets. Now whenever something stops working or has a problem, you'll have the paperwork and all the information at your fingertips, including the customer service number. Always call, even if the warranty is expired. Explain the situation, your purchase details, and then ask one simple question: What can you do for me?

OTHER TIPS

Debit merchandise

Make friends with the managers of your favorite stores, and you might be able to tap into a gold mine. Ask if their "debits" or used merchandise are available for sale. These are items that have been returned but cannot be put back on the floor or returned to the manufacturer. Typically these items are sold for pennies on the dollar.

Hope they won't be undersold

Even though the store where you made a recent purchase doesn't advertise a "we won't be undersold" policy, always take a chance. If, say, the day after you make the purchase, you notice a sale by their competitor during which the same item is offered at 50 percent off, take your purchase back along with the competitor's ad, and simply ask what they can do for you. You'll be surprised what companies will do to keep a customer.

OTHER TIPS

PURCHASES

Share magazine subscriptions

Cut subscription cost by using the buddy system. Find a friend or relative who enjoys the same kinds of magazines and newsletters that you do. Each of you pay half and share it when it arrives each month. Enlarge your group to five: Subscription rates are split four ways; the fifth person receives the issues last, and instead of participating in the price, she becomes the librarian; cataloging, sorting, and storing the publications for the group.

OTHER TIPS

Flowers direct

Before you call a local florist
or a national floral delivery
company to arrange for an out-
of–area delivery, think about
this: These services end up
involving all kinds of middle-
men, which means extra fees
and surcharges for phone calls
and delivery. They usually
have minimums of about $40.00,
and you're never sure what your
recipient will get because you
don't come close to speaking
with the person who will
actually create the arrangement.
You can skip past all of these
extra people by making one call
to a florist in the neighborhood
where your recipient lives.
You'll get three times the
bouquet and service for your
money by dealing directly.

OTHER TIPS

GIFT-GIVING

Everything gifts

Some couples have begun giving an "everything" present to each other for the entire year's gifts (birthday, anniversary, Christmas, etc.) One year the everything gift might be a new computer, or perhaps a piece of home gym equipment recommended by a physical therapist. Not only does it free up the time it takes to purchase gifts all year, couples are not purchasing items for each other that they neither need nor want, just to be buying a gift. A fringe benefit is that the money that is now available at Christmas and throughout the year can now be used to help those less fortunate.

Gift cards

Make your holiday card the gift. Include a family picture, poem, story, original song, or painting, anything of lasting significance.

OTHER TIPS

Group gift

It's not uncommon for children to pool their money to buy gifts for adults, but why not switch that in your family. Instead of everyone buying little gifts for the kids, find out what the kids are asking for (or the parents are requesting for their little ones), pool your resources and get a quality gift, something that will last longer than the box.

Gift stash

Create a gift box in a closet or cupboard into which you can put any free samples you receive, door prizes you win, and gifts you don't like but somebody else might. Always be on the lookout for things to add to your box. When you need a present in a hurry or don't have the cash to spend, go directly to the gift box, and chances are you'll find just the right thing.

OTHER TIPS

GIFT-GIVING

Gift list

Avoid returning unwanted gifts (or pretending you like them) from your spouse or immediate family members by keeping an ongoing record of the things you would like, along with the specific details. Through the year as you see items of particular interest, pick up the store's business card and on the back write the details such as: Red cardigan sweater, brass buttons, wool blend, size eight, $49.98. These cards become a practical gift list that makes gift giving a positive experience for both the giver and receiver.

IOU's

IOU gifts are often the most valuable and appreciated of all. Make up a coupon that is redeemable for something you do well, and tuck it inside a meaningful card. Give what you do best, and you will have given the best gift of all.

OTHER TIPS

Create gift stationery

You can avoid spending if you get into the habit of making your own cards, stationery, postcards, gift bags, etc. You can purchase paper and envelopes in bulk then use the paper cutter at the local copy shop to cut it to the sizes you need. With a few carefully chosen rubber stamps and colored markers, anyone can make beautiful and unique cards and stationery for personal use or to give as gifts. Use postcards whenever possible. This way you'll not only save the cost of the envelope, but the extra postage as well.

Gifts of food

Personalize food gifts with your own decorated label, for example, "Marilyn's Chutney" or "Cathy's Cookies." Attach your recipe and other instructions to the gift with ribbon, raffia, or tasseled cord. Add a spoon or spreader for chutneys or flavored butters.

OTHER TIPS

GIFT-GIVING

Reusable gift containers

Cover gift boxes with appliques, needlework, and quilts, or embroider the recipient's name. These kinds of containers are especially appreciated because they become part of the gift itself. Wrap the box and the lid separately, and the gift box becomes an heirloom to be cherished for years to come.

Homemade gift wrap

Homemade gift wrap is less expensive and much cuter, too! Just wrap any gift inside a brown paper grocery bag and let the kids decorate with their crayons or markers.

Memory quilts

If you've saved lots of your kids' baby clothes and blankets, make quilts for each child from pieces of their old baby clothes.

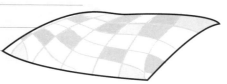

OTHER TIPS

Books

Books make great gifts. But don't limit yourself to shopping in the big bookstore chains. Secondhand bookstores are less expensive and often have out-of-print titles that can't be found in the big chains. Also these store may sell old prints or maps that you could frame for your family members or friends.

Mall alternatives

You can either shop at trendy mall stores for gift items like scented soaps, bath sponges, bath beads, etc., to give as gifts (and spend a small fortune) or you can find reasonable facsimile products; often the exact same thing at discount stores like Wal-Mart, where two bars of scented soap are $2.38 and a "squishy" or sponge is about $2.00.

OTHER TIPS

GIFT-GIVING

Kids' artwork calendars

For all parents who collect hundreds of artwork papers every year and hate to throw them out, here's an excellent gift suggestion: Start collecting large calendars for the New Year from local businesses. Next, select 12 of the most precious pieces of your child's artwork for each calendar and glue them over the printed calendar pictures. (Rubber cement will give excellent results.) This really makes a practical gift that is even more special because of its sentiment. Grandparents, godparents, aunts, and uncles are always delighted; the child is ecstatic with the gift, and the cost is minimal. Finish off the calendar by attaching the child's photograph and autograph.

Just like being there

Make a videotape of your kids. Grandparents, for instance, would love to see them in action, especially if they live some distance away. So instead of capturing a planned and posed session, record the everyday events--everything from bike riding to a live tooth-development demonstration, piano practice to getting ready for bed.

Babysitting coupon

The best gift for parents of little ones is babysitting coupons.

OTHER TIPS

OTHER TIPS

FAMILY CAR

Automobile twins

Even if you have your heart set on a particular vehicle, remember that many cars have twins. General Motors offers many of the same cars as Chevrolets, Buicks, Pontiacs, or Oldsmobiles. Chrysler often clones its cars as Dodges and Plymouths. The annual car issue of *Consumer Reports* tells you which automobiles are twins.

Transferable warranties

If the seller says the vehicle is still under the original manufacturer's warranty or any dealer service contract, double check that these benefits can be transferred from the original owner. Take no one's word for it; read the contracts.

OTHER TIPS

Buyer's Guide sticker

When buying a used car from a dealer, see the Buyer's Guide sticker posted on every used car (for-sale-by-owner cars excluded). It was originated by the Federal Trade Commission as a consumer protection device. For the FTC pamphlet that explains the Buyer's Guide, send 50¢ to: Consumer Information Center-F, P.O. Box 100, Pueblo, CO 81002, and request publication 440T "Buying a Used Car."

Insurance

Check on insurance rates before you make a decision to purchase a particular car. Call your agent with a couple of choices and get quotes.

Dealers' fiscal year

If you are in the market to buy a new car, wait until the end of March. December is not the end of most dealers' fiscal year as most would like you to believe, but March is.

OTHER TIPS

FAMILY CAR

New car test

When you finally take a new car home, give it a long and thorough test-drive. Take the car back immediately if you detect a major problem. The courts have upheld demands for a refund when the car was returned within the first few days.

Ultimate test drive

If you are in the market for a new car, rent one or two of your choices for a weekend when the rental rates are at their lowest. Drive it under a variety of conditions and for long periods of time. A five minute test drive with a hovering dealer sitting in the seat next to you may not give you a true representation of the car's performance and comfort the way a few days on your own will.

OTHER TIPS

Car Seats

Attach the car seat in the back of the car, with the child facing backwards. Never attach the child seat to the front passenger seat if your vehicle is fitted with an airbag. If the air bag opens onto a child safety seat, it will crash against it, capsizing the seat and child inside. When you find a seat you like, try it out! Put your child in the seat and adjust the harnesses and buckles. Make sure it fits in your car.

Seat belts

When your child's ears appear above the level of his car seat, he may be safer in a shoulder or lap seat belt. Do not secure the safety harness under the child's chin; secure it at armpit level.

OTHER TIPS

_____

_____

_____

_____

_____

_____

_____

_____

_____

_____

_____

_____

_____

_____

_____

_____

_____

_____

_____

_____

_____

_____

_____

_____

_____

TRAVEL

Vacation with baby

Can't afford a trip out of town, but want a vacation with your new baby anyway? Turn on the answering machine and tell neighbors and friends your "out" for the weekend. Sleep late, take naps, visit local attractions, tape special moments of baby, and eat special foods you've prepared earlier just for your vacation.

Traveling with kids

When traveling with children give each child a roll of nickels with these instructions: All of these nickels are yours to spend as you like but every time you say "How much farther?" or "Are we there yet?", it will cost you a nickel. This really does the trick.

OTHER TIPS

Pack for fun

A cookie sheet with magnets, Froot Loops™ on a string and egg cartons filled with tiny treats keep little fingers busy. Hang a clear plastic shoe bag on the back of one of the front seats to keep the play gear organized and picked up.

Crayon holders

Empty metal bandage containers make great crayon holders for the family vacation or any on-the-road situation. Small enough to carry in your bag, you can pull out this nifty crayon tote any time you want to keep little hands busy.

Car safety

After you take your toddler out of the car teach him to stand with his back against the door so that he won't run into the street. He'll think it's a game and it's very safe too, until you are ready to take his hand.

OTHER TIPS

TRAVEL

Travel size

Save 35mm film containers for holding face cream, laundry detergent, and other travel supplies you need in small quantities while traveling.

Travel iron

A hair dryer can double as a travel iron. Dampen the creased garment and spread it on a flat surface. Set the dryer on warm and hold it in one hand while smoothing the item with the other.